A WORLD

for Me
and You

Written by
Uju Asika

Illustrated by
Jennie Poh

wren
&rook

Imagine our world in only one colour.
Like the brightest orange
or the most shocking shade of pink!
Can you imagine it?

Or close your eyes and picture
a world with no colours at all.
What would it look like?

Would we dream in black and white?
Maybe every day would feel blank
like a colouring page
when you run out of crayons.

Just imagine ...

Now open your eyes. What can you see?
I see a world alive with colours:
rich earthy browns, deep ocean blues,
sunflower yellow, the black of squid ink.

The average human can see 10 million colours. A tetrochromat is a person who can see ten times that many!

The dappled green of a dewy meadow,
a rainbow at the end of a storm.

My favourite colours of all
are the colours of you and me.
So many wonderful shades
that make up our human family.

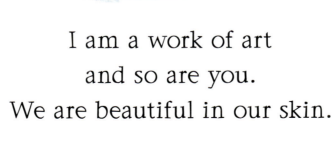

I am a work of art
and so are you.
We are beautiful in our skin.

Imagine our world was one big country
that only had space for someone like me
or someone like you.

Doesn't that sound boring?

Imagine a world with only one face.
The **same face** over and over.
7.9 billion times!

How would we know who was who?

Now look around at all the
many kinds of faces
you can find all over the planet.

Don't you love looking at faces?

Curvy noses, crinkly eyes;
dimpled cheeks,
square jaws and pointy chins.
Freckles, moles and monobrows;
lips that say **ooh**, mouths that say **wow**!
Teeny tiny ears like seashells.

A human face can make at least seven
different expressions! How many expressions
can you make right now?

Faces that are good at keeping secrets
or faces that can never hide
what they're thinking.

And behind every type of face
there is a story of another human
just like you and me.

Imagine a world without flavours
or only one flavour, like ...
hot chilli pepper!
Could you handle it?

Imagine a **world without chocolate**.
Or a whole world full of chocolate:
chocolate houses, chocolate shoes,
chocolate trees, chocolate lakes.
Chocolate **everywhere** ...

until you got sick of it.
What a huge waste!

Now stick out your tongue and let's go
on a flavour hunt around the globe.
What would you like to try?

How about ackee and saltfish
or fluffy Yorkshire pudding?
Big fat balls of fufu with okra soup;
saag aloo with naan bread, pitta dipped in hummus;
slippery noodles wrapped around chopsticks;
hot dogs with sauerkraut spilling out.

Did you know there are 300,000
different plants you can eat on earth?

A steaming pot of slow-cooked stew
with mama's special dumplings.
Your nana's apple pie;
my papa's jollof rice.

Who's hungry?
Come and sit at our table.
Everyone is welcome.

Imagine if the whole world spoke
a different language from you.
How would you get by?
Maybe you wouldn't say a word.

Now open your mouth and say...

ni hao, bonjour, ciao and guten tag.
Hey there, namaste, aloha.
Salaam alaikum, konnichiwa.
Privyet, jambo, kedu, yo.

There are so many ways to say hello,
goodnight, yes please and thank you.
And my favourite of all ...

I love you.

There are at least 6,500
languages spoken across
the world!

And remember:
your name is your first language,
an expression of who you are
from the people who love you most.
So say your name with pride.
Say it with your whole chest!

Imagine the world as a library,
where the doors are open
for anyone to enter
and there is room on the shelves
for everybody's story.

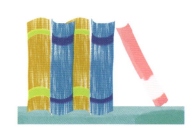

Pull up a chair or sit on the floor;
make yourself at home.
What book shall we choose today?

How about this one –
about a kind and curious child
with a big imagination,
reading all about the wonders
of a world for me and you.

A World for Everyone!

Isn't our world amazing? It's wonderful to see and celebrate so many skin tones, hair styles, languages, beliefs, foods and customs.

Unfortunately, the world is not always kind or fair for everybody.

Here are some ways you can help make things better.

Treat everybody with respect. It's not OK to point, stare, touch or make fun of someone because they seem 'different'. We are all different in one way or another, and that's what makes us special.

The best way to learn about each other is through our stories. They help us understand that we are all unique and we also have lots in common. How many stories of people from different backgrounds can you find to read or listen to?

Be kind and considerate.

That means looking out for other people's feelings and needs. If somebody needs help, lend a hand. If somebody looks sad, offer a smile or a hug. If somebody seems left out, invite them to join in.

Don't be afraid to **ask for help** yourself or to **speak up** when something isn't right. There is always someone who can help.

Did you know that kindness is contagious? If someone is kind to you, it makes you kinder to others. **Practise doing one kind thing** every day.

This can include:

smiling at someone
in the street,

asking someone to play,

helping a neighbour,

sharing your toys
or snacks,

looking after your
environment,

raising money for
a good cause

or opening a door
to let somebody
through.

Kindness opens doors for everyone, including you.
So remember to be kind to yourself too.

To Jed, Ezra and all the other children
who colour the whole world – U.A.

For Barnsbury Primary School
with love – J.P.

First published in Great Britain in 2022 by Wren & Rook

HB ISBN: 978 1 5263 6412 8
PB ISBN: 978 1 5263 6413 5
E-book ISBN: 978 1 5263 6414 2
10 9 8 7 6 5 4 3 2 1

Wren & Rook
An imprint of
Hachette Children's Group
Part of Hodder & Stoughton
Carmelite House
50 Victoria Embankment
London EC4Y 0DZ

An Hachette UK Company
www.hachette.co.uk
www.hachettechildrens.co.uk

Senior Commissioning Editor: Liza Wilde
Art Director: Laura Hambleton
Senior Designer: Sophie Gordon

Printed in China

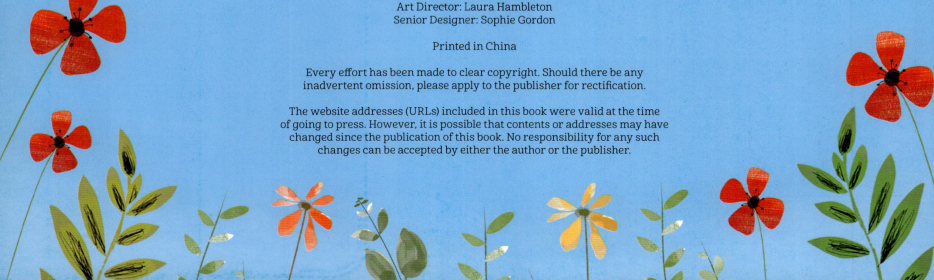